WRITERS

ON

WRITERS

Published in partnership with

WRITERS
STAN
GRANT
ON
THOMAS
KENEALLY
WRITERS

Black Inc.

Published by Black Inc.
in association with the University of Melbourne and State Library Victoria.

Black Inc., an imprint of Schwartz Books Pty Ltd
Level 1, 221 Drummond Street, Carlton VIC 3053, Australia
enquiries@blackincbooks.com
www.blackincbooks.com

State Library Victoria
328 Swanston Street, Melbourne Victoria 3000 Australia
www.slv.vic.gov.au

The University of Melbourne
Parkville Victoria 3010 Australia
www.unimelb.edu.au

9781760642327 (hardback)
9781743821749 (ebook)

A catalogue record for this
book is available from the
National Library of Australia

Cover design by Peter Long and Akiko Chan
Typesetting by Typography Studio
Photograph of Thomas Keneally: University of California
Irvine Public Relations
Photograph of Stan Grant: Tim Bauer

Printed in China by 1010 Printing.

The time is out of joint: O cursèd spite,
That ever I was born to set it right.

Hamlet

HAUNTED

I believe in ghosts; my mother raised me on ghost stories. I would sit with her for hours at night as she told me about the white man on the horse, the old woman of the river, or the small man in the wheelchair who vanished right before her eyes. The world of spirits was so real to us because we lived in a time-between-time: in a world that, at once, was and is. You might call this the Dreaming, but that's probably a bit exotic for the way I was raised.

The anthropologist William Stanner added an elusive, elegiac quality to this time-between-time with his neologism the 'everywhen'. Stanner captured a timelessness that befits our haunted land. And that's the word for me: *haunted*. It is not possible to sit in the still of this place we now call Australia and not be alive to all that has happened here. I was back on my father's ancestral country recently and I felt it again – that moan that comes from the earth, especially when the light dims and people retreat back into the darkness.

Alone in this land, I know that time doesn't move in a straight line. Like the distant call of birds or other animals, time itself echoes. There's a different sound at night; it is the sound of absence. How could it not be? For tens of thousands of years, our earth and everything that lived and breathed on it heard the sound of a people, the rhythm of their speech, the patter of their feet coming and going on the ground, their songs and ceremony, and then, in what is in the span of humanity just the blink of an eye – there was silence. In a generation or two, my people were nearly extinguished. What does that do to a place? To lose its people and to witness unspeakable crimes. I think our country grieves, and in that grief a profound sadness remains. The lost souls form the spirit of the land itself. Mum was right: there are ghosts.

*

Before starting this essay, I went in search of a ghost: the ghost of Jimmy Governor. I went to the place where he took his last breath. The old Darlinghurst Gaol is now the site of the National Art School. The gallows are gone. But behind the high sandstone walls, it is not so hard to imagine what it was like, back then. I was taken through the time-worn corridors, past what once were cold prison cells. I turned a corner and stopped suddenly, like something – or someone – had grabbed hold of me. I looked up and my tour guide said, that's where it happened. Exactly there, she said, where I was standing, is where Jimmy was hanged. Above me was where the trapdoor would have been, and where the hangman would have placed the noose around Jimmy's neck.

Jimmy Governor was executed at 9 a.m. on 18 January 1901. The newspaper reported that he had slept well, had a good breakfast and walked to his death smoking a cigarette. A priest walked with him. Jimmy took the cigarette from his mouth; threw it away before the white hood covered his face. He tilted his neck – just slightly – to make it easier for the hangman to attach the noose. Death was instantaneous. There was hardly a tremor in the body, the reporter wrote. Jimmy Governor's clothes were burned. He was buried beyond the prison walls.

Jimmy Governor killed children. He killed women. He took an axe to a family and then went on a rampage of theft, rape and murder. Nine people, he slaughtered – for slaughter it was. The most hunted man in the country. A man could earn himself a fortune for shooting Jimmy dead. Jimmy fantasised about being a bushranger like Ned Kelly. Ned was his hero. They shared some things in common: they were poor, rejected and exploited. But Jimmy's image doesn't lend itself to kitsch art and souvenirs. He would never be remembered like Ned. Jimmy belonged to the wretched of our earth – people Australia hoped would disappear, or be bred out.

Jimmy left no last words, not like Ned. 'Such is life': did Ned really say that? Does it matter? There's a nation in those words. Ned gave us poetry and a philosophy: a devil-may-care stoicism. In death, Ned's Irish Catholic rebelliousness is de-fanged, smoothed out until it becomes just a roguish charm: a Heath Ledger wink. But Jimmy Governor's is a brooding presence and he leaves us in silence; there are no final words. He leaves behind a space for storytellers, and Jimmy is a tantalising subject. Jimmy's epitaph is ours to write.

From our vantage point, Jimmy lived and died at the crossroads of history: he marked a moment between the old and the new. Between what was and what is yet to be: time-between-time. In books and film, storytellers have sought to cast

Jimmy's life and crimes as a morality play or a *cri de coeur*. Australia – its brutal treatment of Aboriginal people – has been put on trial as much as Jimmy himself. What Jimmy did was monstrous, barbaric; no provocation could justify his violence. I know that is the correct moral reaction to the murder of innocent people, but I can't let it rest there because he was pushed to this insanity, there is no doubt about that: cheated, humiliated and belittled. His white wife – a white wife, what was he thinking! – was scorned and laughed at for 'living with savages'.

That's what draws us to this story: not just the crime, but what the crime represents. Jimmy Governor has stood in for every one of my ancestors, and he put a face to my own rage. To me, conscious as I am of my family's suffering, Jimmy's execution has resonated not as an example of justice done, but as a reminder of the times that justice went undone – the slaughter of black people that was never prosecuted. No one is innocent. The story becomes a symbol of a ritual cleansing for a nation born in blood and murder: white blood and black blood smeared in one more act of a brutal frontier before we proclaimed a new nation.

Jimmy was executed less than three weeks after Federation, and here I am searching for him still, looking back into the past to try to make sense of who I am. More than a hundred years later, Jimmy Governor still casts a shadow over this nation. Jimmy Governor haunts me and he haunts Australia. This is a ghost story as Jacques Derrida would have seen it. He was on to something when he coined the word 'hauntology', to describe how the traces of our past – our ghosts – throw shadows on our world. It is a tear in time, a crack in the fortress of modernity. The West thinks it can vanquish history; that the past can be entombed. History, we are told, is an arc of progress that bends towards freedom, and each generation shakes itself loose from the grip of its ancestors.

There is an end to history, so it is said – not that time stops or that past events or people cease to matter, but that we win our freedom. Triumphant Western liberals declared victory after the fall of the Berlin Wall in 1989. Francis Fukuyama proclaimed the battle of ideology settled: liberal democracy alone was humanity's final destination. It is a seductive idea; liberalism takes us over the horizon where we can see a future that is ours to make, unconstrained by tyrants or faith or race. It is an idea that the West claims as its own, something the philosopher Hegel called the 'absolute spirit', where master and slave are each freed from the chains of the oppressed and the oppressor. Whatever its sins – and there are many – liberalism contains the promise of liberty. To paraphrase Pascal Bruckner, it is a jailer, that's true, but one who slips you the key.

*

So why am I here, standing outside Jimmy Governor's cell? What is the pull of the past, and what is so lacking now that I have to go in search of a ghost? The battlegrounds of liberalism are littered with corpses; that's what Derrida sensed after 1989, when he saw the dead rising and bringing their history with them. He was right. Look around us: history didn't end. In fact, the Cold War itself may have been a momentary slumber – a break from catastrophic hostility – and the fall of the wall served only to wake us up again. History is back, and with it its twin: identity. It is an identity forged in a memory of grievance that vows revenge. Toxic identity has set our world ablaze – democracy bends to tyranny, and the bonds of civility are severed. In the United States, supposedly a beacon of democracy, identity conflicts across race, class and culture have made the country almost ungovernable. The political scientist Mark Lilla has called these seething, angry identity tribes the 'shipwrecked minds', who see no future but only the past floating by like debris from a wreck. It is the past they cling to, to recover old glory, to make themselves great again. Fukuyama may yet be right: liberal democracy could be our best hope for freedom, but first it must survive.

This is what Jimmy Governor has been to me: the memory of a wound. He is a scar on our history that runs like a fault line between black and white. Coming to the place of his execution is like a pilgrimage. It is an impossible burden to place on a dead man I never knew. But my life has wrapped around his for as long as I can remember. Jimmy was the bogeyman of my childhood. My grandfather used to scare me by warning that Jimmy was waiting out in the scrub. If I was naughty, Jimmy would come for me. Jimmy Governor grew up with Wiradjuri people; his own heritage is less clear. Our families were deeply linked: we came from the same country; the same history; the same missions. We were born on the fringes of this new Australia in the late nineteenth century. We had the surnames of the invaders: Grant, Naden, Simpson,

Gray, Knight, Reid or Towney. They are quint-essentially white names – all that we inherited from our white forefathers, who slipped across the colour line at night and then abandoned their black kids at dawn.

We were a new breed of people: blacks. Not the same Aborigines who were here before the First Fleet, but not white either. We sang Christian hymns and played cards, drank grog and strummed guitars to old cowboy songs. I have a photo from Bulgandramine Mission, at Peak Hill in the central west of New South Wales, of all of my mob, dressed up to the nines for a mission wedding. The women in long dresses, the men in coats and starched collars. There in the middle of the photo is my great Aunty Kate – my grandfather's sister – then a young girl, and standing next to her is the dark, unsmiling face of Tommy Governor – Jimmy's brother.

There's another little twist in my family tree. Jimmy's white wife, Ethel, moved to the South

Coast after Jimmy's execution. She had a young child and was looking for a new beginning. Ethel Page had crossed a line from one Australia to another and could never go back. White Australia had no place for her. Whatever her fate would be, it would be with the blacks. Ethel met another Aboriginal man, settled down with him and had several more children. One of her grandchildren married my father's sister. Their children – my cousins – are a blood connection to a night of violence that shook this country to the core and for a moment raised the very real fear that Jimmy Governor had launched a race war.

Jimmy Governor is not a name in a history book – he is as vivid to me as any of the ghosts in my mother's stories. It is my worst impulses that draw me to him; this resentment, or, as Friedrich Nietzsche would have called it, 'ressentiment', an all-consuming historical fever. The man of ressentiment, said Nietzsche, 'loves hidden crannies, tortuous paths and backdoors'. History is a festering sore to be picked at over and over, never allowed it to heal. Jimmy Governor was a grotesque murderer who took an axe to the skulls of children, I know he is beyond sympathy . . . and yet.

I can never get one image out of my mind, when I think of Jimmy Governor. It is taken from the diary of one of the wardens who guarded Jimmy's cell. In the prisoner's last days, the warden wrote, Jimmy alternated between singing native songs and reading aloud passages from the Bible. What a vision. Mythic. Poignant. Poetic. Cinematic. To the storyteller it is profound: a man between sin and redemption, between a Christian god and the spirits of his ancestors. It reads like the final scene of a film. The distant sound of didgeridoo and clapsticks, a nasal, droning voice, a lament in a language itself facing death as surely as the prisoner. Cut to a man on his knees, hands folded in prayer: 'Thy kingdom come, thy will be done . . .' A cross nailed askew to the cell wall. Close-up of a prison warden's eyes through a keyhole.

There, in Jimmy's cell, is the struggle for my own identity: I exist somewhere between the Enlightenment and the Dreaming; propelled by progress and liberalism and yet also reaching back to keep a hold on something eternal. God, sin and redemption, black and white, war and peace: this is what drew Thomas Keneally to Jimmy Governor. Like me, he has peered through the keyhole into Jimmy's cell searching for something of himself and his country. Jimmy haunts Tom as he haunts me, as he haunts our country. He is the spectre that will not let us bury our history; he holds modernity – its promise of freedom and liberty – just out of reach.

'What does it mean to follow a ghost?' Derrida asked. 'And what if this came down to being followed by it, always, persecuted perhaps by the very chase we are leading?' The future, Derrida said, 'comes back in advance: from the past, from the back'. We have 'the bread of apocalypse in our mouths'. This is the bitter aftertaste of my history, returning again and again. It has a hold on me that must be put right if I am to live free of it. When I considered writing this essay, there was only one book to choose: Thomas Keneally's *The Chant of Jimmie Blacksmith*. It is the book that speaks to this time out of joint, and it has been with me since I began to ask questions about my place in the world and wonder whether, in the words of Derrida, I would always be late to the end of history.

INVISIBLE MAN

'Yes, boss. No, boss. Three bags full, boss.'
My brother and I used to tease our mother with this little routine. Mock blackfella voices. Playing the subservient good Aborigine.

'I'll be a good blackfella for you, boss.'

'I'm not like those other blacks. I got a good job. I got a house. I got a wife – she white too, boss.'

Mum used to scold us: 'Stop it or you will end up talking like that.' She didn't like us mocking our own people. But she'd laugh too. Because in our own way we were mocking white people. Our script was straight out of *The Chant of Jimmie Blacksmith* – the movie, not the book. We saw the movie first. I must have been about fifteen when I watched it. The same age that I entered, truly entered, the white world.

We had moved to Canberra from my hometown of Griffith. Dad got a job in a sawmill. It was the pattern of our lives, being constantly on the move. My childhood was a blur: one small town after another. But Canberra felt like a foreign country, bigger than any place I had lived. And white. To me, Canberra seemed like the whitest place on the planet. Imagine: I had gone from being surrounded by other Aboriginal people – my family, cousins, friends – to this, where my sister and I were the only black kids in the school. I had no idea who these people were. I didn't get their jokes; I didn't understand how they spoke to one another. I was uncertain of everything: I didn't even know how to eat around them. They talked about food I had never heard of. Seriously, I studied white kids to see how I might fit in; watched what they ate, where they sat and how they interacted with each other.

I don't think I had ever spent time in a white person's house – dirt-poor whites, perhaps, those who lived alongside us, but not these white people, kids whose fathers came home from work clean and who had lived in the same houses all their lives and had the same friends from childhood. The smart-arse racist remarks started on day one, so I had a choice: I could fight my way from one day to the next, or I could shut up and get along. I swallowed my pride, laughed at their jokes and shrank a little bit inside. I learned what every Aboriginal person – every black or non-white person – learns: we don't make the rules and we don't have the power.

The Chant of Jimmie Blacksmith came along at the right time for me. Director Fred Schepisi called it the chant of the underdog: a man pushed too far. Jimmie was half-white and married to a white woman – a proper Christian wedding, he said – and he worked at local farms. He did all the things white people told him he had to do but he was cheated, humiliated and insulted. He hit back by slaughtering a white farming family who had taunted him and his wife. It was a powerful but brutal film, too much for white audiences then, and if it was made today I suspect it would be too much still.

Schepisi made a war movie. Jimmie wasn't taking revenge on just a family – he took revenge on a nation, and I cheered. When he brought his axe down on the head of a farmer's wife, I felt my heart leap. Sickening, I know, that anyone could be exhilarated by murder, but that's what I was meant to feel, just like John Wayne killing the Indians thrilled white audiences. Schepisi's Jimmie was a hero I had never seen before. White people always had power over our lives, imposing it by force, stealing our land and killing our people. Now Jimmie was taking that power back.

Jimmie declared war on white Australia and deep in me, masked from the white kids I had to befriend just to get by, was a sullen hatred at everything Australia was. I had filed away every slight and insult. Every time I cringed about being black. All the shame I felt. I saw how hard Mum and Dad worked for pitiful pay; I saw the sadness and the worry in Dad's eyes; I watched Mum stretch mince and onions to feed four kids and whoever else happened to be living with us; I had to wear other people's discarded clothes; I didn't have money for the tuckshop; we didn't have a home, so we had to keep moving; when I visited my great-grandmother on the mission at Griffith, I saw mangy dogs and broken glass and I knew who put us there. We didn't have a choice in this. This was what was left after invasion and massacre and poisoning and disease and what Australia likes to call 'dispossession', a cynical word that avoids telling the truth of what it is: theft.

I entered the world of white Australia as an invisible man. In the words of Ralph Ellison: 'people refuse to see me'. People like me wonder if we are not phantoms ourselves – ghosts. Ellison said we want to be real, that we ache with the need to convince ourselves that we exist. But we are just figments of the imagination: in Ellison's case, of the white imagination. We appear only in the inner eyes of those who look upon us. They can't see us as we truly are, so they invent us – not fully human, but something that resembles human. Aboriginal people only come into view when they become something white people recognise. I have lived this transformation: from a black boy among other black boys, to the only black boy in a white school, to a black boy on white television. With each incarnation I became more visible – more 'real' – until now I am deemed worthy of the great white compliment: 'but you're not like the others'.

So we have a choice, Ellison said, to strike out violently against those blind others until they cannot deny us (but that, he reminded us, is seldom successful), or to embrace our invisibility and

'walk softly so as not to awaken the sleeping ones'.
James Baldwin read Ellison and I read Baldwin
and I listened when he said he had spent a life-
time 'watching white people and outwitting them
so that I might survive'. We can even convince
others that we are not black. Not that we stop
being black or 'pass' as white; but as in a magic
trick the audience wants to be convinced: they
see what they want to see. As Ellison wrote, 'it is
possible to carry on a fight against them without
their realising it'.

The invisible man exists on the fringes of
modernity. He is a man without history, as Hegel
would have seen it. He does not appear until he is
discovered and will forever be measured against
his discoverer. Yet the invisible man desperately
wants to be seen. Violence, subterfuge, mockery
and performance: all of these are in his trick bag,
and, as with the magician, success depends on
allowing the audience to see what they want to
see. That's what my brother and I were doing

playing our scenes from *The Chant of Jimmie Blacksmith*: we were performing the Aborigine whom Australia could recognise.

Jimmie Blacksmith is Thomas Keneally's invisible man. He is no longer Jimmy Governor. Keneally's Jimmie is stripped of Governor's complexity. He is a paler facsimile; a parody. Governor was defiant and proud – he was known to say he was 'as good as a white man' – the son of two Aboriginal parents: his father, Tommy, wore the chest scars of a tribally initiated man; his mother, Annie, the daughter of an Aboriginal woman and an Irish stockman. Jimmie, however, is an often obsequious half-caste; at times a grinning Stepin Fetchit, bowing and scraping for a white man's approval, lusting after the fat wives of white farmers, then brooding with resentment at each rejection or insult. It is his own blackness Jimmie seems to despise, as much, if not more than, the whites. Jimmie wants to get as far away as possible from his black family, telling the

Methodist missionary: 'That mob make me feel sick, Mr Neville.' It is another example of how Keneally fails to see who we are. His Jimmie must escape his blackness to seek acceptance from the whites, and there is no doubt some Aboriginal people made those choices. But there is nothing in the real Jimmy Governor's life to suggest that he despised himself or his people.

It is true that Jimmy Governor also wanted to live in the white world – more than that, he demanded the right to – and at his trial in 1900, he said he was 'never a loafer like some other blackfellows', but don't mistake that for hating who he was. In their finely researched book *The True Story of Jimmy Governor*, Laurie Moore and Stephan Williams make it very clear he was 'brought up to work hard'; he had a 'fierce sense of independence' and life on the mission 'living from hand to mouth' alongside his own people 'broken in spirit' convinced him that 'he would work for wages, not rations and handouts'. In contrast to the fictional Jimmie Blacksmith, who blames the blacks for their state, Moore and Williams point out that the treatment of his people by the whites 'strengthened Jimmy's reaction against injustice and paternalism'. Jimmy didn't want to be white; he refused to be a white man's image of an Aborigine.

I feel I know Jimmy – the man Moore and Williams describe could be my father, a man who would not buckle to the white world, ferociously proud of being a Wiradjuri man. Dad got us off the missions – as did his father before him – opting for life on the margins rather than life under the thumb, but we never forgot who we were. Keneally's caricature of a self-loathing Jimmie Blacksmith is a lost opportunity to explore the complex ways that Aboriginal people – just like my family or the Governor family – were pushing against a white world that would not accept them for who they were; that would not see them as equal; that, in truth, would not see them as human.

Tom Keneally could not possibly understand Jimmy Governor – as he could not possibly comprehend my father – so he invented his own Aborigine: Jimmie Blacksmith. Tom is an outsider – he has said that is the reason he writes – and in Jimmie he creates the archetypal outsider. I don't think I'm wrong in seeing black Jimmie as Irish Tom's mirror image: swap Fenian grievance for Aboriginal resentment, the Dreaming for Catholic ritual, and Indigenous sovereignty for Irish republicanism. Jimmie Blacksmith is a memory without memory, a faint trace of the real Jimmy Governor, now existing in the inner eye of the white author who can't see him as anything more than a man trapped between worlds. Keneally's Jimmie Blacksmith is stripped of modernity's great promise: progress. Jimmie is a man without telos.

THE BEAUTIFUL SOUL

In June of 1900 Jimmie Blacksmith's
maternal uncle Tabidgi – Jackie Smolders
to the white world – was disturbed to get
news that Jimmie had married a white girl
in the Methodist church at Wallah.

Therefore he set out with Jimmie's
initiation tooth to walk a hundred miles to
Wallah. The tooth would be a remonstration
and lay a tribal claim on Jimmie.

Thomas Keneally,

The Chant of Jimmie Blacksmith

From this opening of Keneally's novel, Jimmie Blacksmith is doomed. He is a man denied the right of becoming. It is terrible to rob someone of becoming because it robs them of a future; they remain frozen in time, unable to change. To embrace becoming is to embrace freedom: to hold two or more thoughts at once; to change one's mind; to choose love outside faith or race. As the philosopher Charles Taylor writes in *Sources of the Self*: 'Modern freedom was won by our breaking loose from older moral horizons.' Jimmie's life is not modern: it is mechanical; an endless extraction of difference until all difference is subordinated to some assigned identity. This identity is the enemy of freedom: a choking, stifling identity that kills. Gilles Deleuze calls this the death of the 'beautiful soul' – the beautiful soul who says, 'We are different but not opposed.'

The beautiful soul balances the tension in modernity: that of tradition and progress. Without tradition we are rootless, restless souls estranged from kin and community, divorced from faith and meaning. Without progress we are rooted in place, bound to a deadening conformity, unable or even prohibited to think new thoughts.

Tradition holds us back and progress leaves us untethered: alienated.

At the risk of disappearing down a philosophical rabbit hole, I note that Deleuze was speaking back to Hegel, to the German philosopher's idea of 'negation'. For Deleuze, Hegel's belief in mutual recognition sought to erase difference. It is the struggle of the master and the slave, each locked in a battle from which they will be relieved only when they no longer have need of the other. But what is left? Deleuze says that to Hegel 'difference remains subordinated to identity'. Deleuze's beautiful soul 'behaves like a justice of the peace thrown onto a field of battle'. History, he says, is made 'through bloody contradictions' but the beautiful soul 'sees differences everywhere and appeals to them only as respectable, reconcilable'. In crude terms, Hegel favours an assimilationist model where we sublimate our differences in some greater state, and Deleuze an integrationist model of retaining difference without being chained to it. In any case, these are the great philosophical debates of modernity that writers like Tom Keneally cannot imagine Aboriginal people being part of.

For Jimmie Blacksmith cannot make these choices: he is locked out of modernity itself. For Keneally, there is no beautiful soul in Jimmie. As far as modernity is concerned, Jimmie is bound for extinction. When Tabidgi arrives with his initiation tooth, Jimmie is already dead: there remains only time between him and the hangman. The rupture has taken place; a crack has opened in the moral universe: Jimmie has married a white girl and, what's more, in a Methodist church. Tabidgi knows the initiation tooth lays a claim on his nephew from which Jimmie cannot escape. Yet even then Tabidgi's magic is fading; the world has no place for his tribal ritual. Initiation ceremonies themselves will soon cease and Tabidgi will be just Jackie Smolders to the white world.

*

Let me say something here about Keneally the writer. This opening is astonishing in its brevity, and its depth. Keneally is a master. The ideas and the juxtaposition of worlds: the pervading doom; the hint of the violence to come and the crushing inevitability of modernity that is contained in these few sentences is inspiring and daunting. He sets a bar few writers can meet and he does it with no flash. There are no tricks here. Keneally has no need to impress us with a frothy, frilly command of language. The writing is mundane and perfunctory, yet it is as simple and powerful an opening as 'Once upon a time'. It puts me in mind of Orwell, another writer who makes the craft seem so simple that anyone could do it . . . until they try.

'It was a bright cold day in April, and the clocks were striking thirteen.'

Like the clocks in Orwell's *Nineteen Eighty-Four*, Jimmie's tooth is out of place and out of time and the world itself is on a tilt.

*

If there is a 'beautiful soul' in Tom's book, it is the white girl Jimmie has married. She is free to choose in a way that Jimmie isn't. She will pay a price – insult, pity – for marrying Jimmie, but hers is not an existential crisis. She is assuredly white, yet free to see difference and love him anyway. As a white person, her place in the world is secure in ways Jimmie's can never be. Jimmie is constantly told that if he has children they will be just one-quarter black, and their kids one-eighth, until they are scarcely black at all. This is the deal: we become more visible to white people – more fit for modernity – as we progressively 'disappear'. And yet, there is always the 'stain' – as Jimmie is told by his employer Mr Newby, whose family Jimmie will slaughter: 'It doesn't matter how many times yer descendants bed down, they'll never get anything that don't have the tarbrush in it. And it'll always spoil 'em.'

Deleuze says 'modern thought is born . . . of the loss of identities'. It is in that loss – that void between the need to belong and the yearning to be free – that we do our worst to each other. *The Chant of Jimmie Blacksmith* is a meditation on modernity: its promise, its price and whom it encompasses. The Irish character, Toban – part of the posse hunting the fugitive Jimmie – undoubtedly belongs. The Irish may well have been the 'blacks of Europe', but for all the brutality of Cromwellian conquest they are still part of the great sweep of progress – that human drive for freedom that Hegel said propelled history itself. Toban bemoans the 'victims of tyrannous British eviction' without a moment's reflection that the British had done the same to the man he was now pursuing. Because in this new land, Toban is a white man. The colony is on the verge of becoming a nation: 'We're going t' be a bloody power in the world,' he says. Toban's grandparents 'all had the arse out of their trousers. Out here we live like kings in Australia.'

Jimmie Blacksmith learns too that possession is 'a holy state' in Australia. It is the measure of human existence: 'Jimmie's criteria were: home, hearth, wife, land. Those who possessed these had beatitude unchallengeable.'

Poor Jimmie: he thinks he can purchase his soul, but the opposite is true: to live in this white world, he has to sell his soul. He joins the police as a tracker and is given an ill-fitting cast-off uniform: 'a comic abo in some other black's clothes'. Comic he is, but Jimmie thinks he is official now, 'a registered, accredited, uniformed black man'. And he is dangerous. Now he has authority to crack black heads, to smash everything he had come from, and he takes to it with glee. He can punish black people for being black.

There is no reward for Jimmie: not even love. The white woman, Gilda, whom he marries, is a giggling fool already pregnant with the child of a white cook. (In Fred Schepisi's film, Keneally plays the role of the cook, which strikes me as perverse – as though not content with having created such a hollow, weak character, he has to add another personal layer of humiliation.) Gilda was not what Jimmie had hoped for but the best he could attain – another marker of his lowly place in the world. Keneally can't allow Jimmie the gift of love for the same reason Jimmie can't truly exist: 'For he was a hybrid.' The white blood in him meant he had no claim on the spiritual love of the tribe, and his black blood denied him the joys of romantic love.

> Suspended between the loving tribal life and the European rapture from on high called falling in love . . . Jimmie Blacksmith held himself firm and soundly despised as many people as he could.

Goethe told us there is no remedy but love for the great superiority of others. It is a hard thought to get my head around: must I acquiesce to power – love it, indeed? Especially power that comes from force. But then isn't that what Martin Luther King Jr did? His love was the greatest power of all. It is not the power that others hold over us that destroys our souls; it is the absence of love. There is no love in Keneally's novel. The blacks are deformed by the lack of love. The women especially are loathsome, degraded creatures: TB-riddled, coughing, heaving; vomiting wenches; 'gins' and 'lubras' who Jimmie takes refuge in, then despises (and himself even more) for having done so. Jimmie himself was conceived out of lust and violence, the product of 'a visit some white man had made to Brentwood blacks' camp'. And the weak, vile black men in Tom's novel sell their women for the price of rum.

I have to say the way Keneally writes about black women disturbs me. He seems to reserve a special venom for them. They are contemptible creatures. I know he is reflecting the times in which the book is set, when white men preyed on black women, but I can't help recoiling from the language. Black women sing 'shrieking welcomes' to the 'white phallus, powerful demolisher of tribes'. Jimmie lies down 'with a scrawny gin called Florence' who, Keneally writes, 'barked and barked and dredged blood from beneath her lips'. Compare that to how Keneally describes a white woman whom Jimmie sees passing by, who 'had an aura of being delicate' with fat acquiescent lips, distant eyes; 'full and ripe', she is Jimmie's fantasy: 'a symbol, a state of blessedness'. By contrast, the black women are the work of the devil: immoral vessels, devoid of any virtue and dwelling in the worst of rooms of hell. I want to extend to Tom the rights of literary licence, but I am horrified and offended at the way he describes women who could have been my great-grandmothers. I knew my great-grandmother and I have photos of black women of that time, women of dignity and bearing. They bear no resemblance to the vile, wanton, rutting wenches of Tom's novel.

*

Where there is no love, there is no God. In the 'chaos of black-white meanness', God has forsaken Jimmie's world. The black mission Verona, a place of drunken men and lascivious women, obsessed and frightened Jimmie; it was a place that had fallen from God's eye: 'Jimmie Blacksmith would willingly have burned Verona off the map'. Jimmie is a missionary black and God has not redeemed his soul; he has divided it. A fugitive killer on the run with his 'full blood' Aborigine brother, Mort, Jimmie kidnaps a schoolteacher, who reminds Jimmie of the 'truth' of who he is: 'The boy isn't really your brother. He's an aborigine, Jimmie. Not like you. There's too much Christian in you, Jimmie, and it will only bugger him up. Like it's buggered you.'

Mort, like Tabidgi, is the Aborigine whom history has now overtaken. Keneally valorises the noble savage even as — or even because — he does not question the inevitability of the

Aborigines' extinction. It is the price of modernity. If there is a place in heaven for Jimmie's victims, Jimmie himself is condemned to purgatory: 'Mr Jimmie Blacksmith, mighty terroriser, lost beyond repair somewhere between the Lord God of Hosts and the shrunken cosmogony of his people.'

Jimmie's world is a world of shadows; he is defined by what he is not – not white, not truly black – rather than what he is. The author, Keneally, breathes life into Jimmie and what existence the fictional character has extends only beyond the tip of Keneally's pen. Where is the real Jimmy Governor? Jimmy loved: he married a white woman who loved him; his child was his child, not the offspring of a white cook. Jimmy went to church, read the Bible, played cricket – none of this made him less of an Aborigine. This same Jimmy took an axe to white women and children and then went to the gallows in prayer. What a fascinating, horrifying, complex character he is: too complex, too real for Tom Keneally. Keneally cannot even bring himself to use Jimmy's real name; he turns him into Jimmie Blacksmith, the writer's own invention.

Keneally cannot extend to Jimmy Governor the same fullness of existence that he gives to his most famous 'creation', Oskar Schindler. The member of the Nazi party and saviour of so many Jews can live on the page with all his contradiction, all of his humanity and his name. Schindler contends with the bureaucratic philosophical nightmare of Nazism, and exercises his freedom. Keneally can see in Oskar Schindler what he can't see in Jimmy Governor: a man of modernity. He can't tell the story he wants to tell with Jimmy Governor, so he invents his own Aborigine.

Historian Bob Reece says Aborigines 'were both an invention and product of European colonisation'. There were no 'Aborigines' here until white people arrived and named us. Hundreds of different peoples or tribes, or nations as we now call them, were produced in the white imagination as a homogenous group. Aborigines became part of a national narrative: the noble savage fading from the frontier; the doomed race. By the time Keneally invented Jimmie Blacksmith in 1972, the narrative was changing. This was a time of anti-Vietnam protests, the election of the Whitlam Labor government and the Aboriginal Tent Embassy: Keneally was writing from the age against an age. Jimmie Blacksmith was now a symbol of protest: a mirror to reflect Australia's shame and guilt for its treatment of Aboriginal people. As Bob Reece says:

> The old orthodoxy that European occupation of the Australian continent was essentially peaceful (that the Aborigines 'simply faded away') has been replaced by a new orthodoxy. We are now told that Aboriginal reaction

to the European presence was characterised by 'resistance', indeed, that it is maintained today by Aboriginal activists and groups seeking land rights. The broken black figures in our city parks should not be seen as 'alcoholic derelicts' but as 'patriots' passively resisting the European lifestyle.

Angry at his repeated rejections, Keneally's Jimmie Blacksmith wonders if he should 'declare war' on the whites who have wronged him: will they then see him as an equal? Is this how the real Jimmy Governor saw the world? His biographers do say Jimmy's mother had raised him on stories of how the white man had stolen the Aborigines' land. No doubt she did; I grew up hearing the same. But they stress there is no evidence to suggest that his murders were vengeance for the wrongs of history. At his trial, Jimmy made no mention of historical injustice or avenging white domination. He said he was goaded into the killings by his uncle and brother. He testified that his wife was taunted 'for marrying a blackfellow'. He said, 'That made me very wild, so we went and killed them.' Rather than hatred of the whites, Jimmy again says he was as good as any white man, that he 'always worked, and paid for what I got'. But Keneally was writing a protest story for a protest era; he needed Jimmie Blacksmith to be the freedom fighter that Jimmy Governor never was. Jimmy was a man who wanted respect. He bridled against injustice, yes, but this was a crime of anger, not an act of war.

Albert Camus wrote of the absurdity of the world that 'the absurd becomes God . . . and that inability to understand becomes the existence that illuminates everything'. Absurdity is truth, and, in their inability to understand, white authors like Tom reveal the limits of my own existence. He is not alone. William Stanner, the anthropologist who gave us the phrase 'The Great Australian Silence' to describe how Aborigines had been written out of history, did as much as anyone to fix in the Australian imagination the idea that Aboriginal people would shatter at the touch of modernity. He idealised traditional tribal society and feared – not entirely unreasonably – the upheaval that the coming of the whites would continue to bring.

Of course people suffered, of course it was devastating. But I read Stanner or I read Kenneally and I disappear – my family disappears – they create us as they see us: doomed. But we were stockmen and cooks and drovers and we worked on the roads and we picked fruit and now we are doctors and lawyers and carpenters and priests and journalists and writers like me; we didn't vanish, we weren't crushed: we survived. The noble savage or the doomed race or the resistance warrior; none of it illuminates everything, but to reduce us to a simple narrative steals our souls.

When I was sixteen and finding my way in a foreign place, angry and uncertain, Keneally gave me a myth to live by. When I watched Fred Schepisi's film and heard the actor Tom E. Lewis as Jimmie Blacksmith say, 'Tell 'em I declared war,' it filled me with pride. I heard the voices of all of my ancestors. And yet. Must I cleave to the memory of wounds? When narrative – any single narrative – frames identity, I feel the walls close in on me. When history is an unending battlefield, I cannot find peace. Is there truth and justice? When do we put away the weapons of memory? I don't know; these are questions I am still asking and likely always will.

Keneally leaves these big questions alone: all he has to offer me is a doomed warrior and an eternal wound. I need more than that.

Keneally has what Deleuze calls 'a sense for cruelty or a taste for destruction'. The author does not see difference; he sees affirmation proceeding from negation. Let me explain: for Jimmie to be seen, to be acknowledged, he must accept what he is not. He is not white, and he is told he is not truly black. To achieve affirmation, Jimmie must assume 'the weight of that which is denied and negation itself'. Deleuze says there are two ways to deal with 'necessary destructions': 'that of the poet, who speaks in the name of a creative power to affirm Difference . . . and that of the politician, who is above all concerned to deny that which "differs", so as to conserve or prolong an established historical order'. Keneally here is the politician, not the poet. Jimmie's 'difference' is his death. He is sacrificed to an 'historical order' that Keneally accepts implicitly, even as he uses Jimmie to rail against it.

Hegel – who so influenced, inspired and challenged Deleuze, as he does me – said we begin our journey when we are 'utterly torn asunder'. Jimmy Governor and I come from a rupture in time when modernity tore our world asunder. He sought what I seek today, to live in the world with all of its horror or its beauty; to live with my history and find joy anyway. I have shared Jimmy's anger, but have survived the worst of it. Jimmy sought to live in modernity. What choice did he have? He sought it in love – genuine love – and faith and the belief he was 'as good as any white man'. That isn't Keneally's Jimmie Blacksmith. I can't help but feel that what Keneally has created is an imitation of a white man who met only humiliation and despised as many as he could.

I can't explain Jimmy Governor's violence; I have only Jimmy's words at his trial, and they aren't enough. To take an axe to women and children – crimes so monstrous can't easily be explained. On that awful night he was taunted to the point of madness, his wife had been insulted and she threw that back at Jimmy; she challenged his manhood. He had been cheated before; short-changed; and he had tried to escape the misery of the missions that he had been raised on. All of this would have been coursing through him on that night. He went to the door of the home-stead to demand the food rations that were his due, and there was an axe and all it took was a moment of rage.

Tom Keneally wanted to see an act of war, to write a story of resistance, but Jimmy Governor – in all his complexity; in his humanity; in his modernity – wouldn't let him, so he invented Jimmie Blacksmith and he wrote a novel so powerful that he made Jimmie Blacksmith more real to me than the real thing.

THE WHITE GAZE

Civilisation did not begin in Australia until
the last quarter of the eighteenth century.

Manning Clark, *History of Australia*

Toni Morrison had to confront a reality that all non-white people have to confront: 'Our lives have no meaning, no depth without the white gaze.' Of course our lives have meaning to us, but Morrison was talking about how the white gaze has held power over us, and it was Morrison's struggle to live beyond it, 'to think about how free I can be as an African-American woman writer in my genderised, sexualised, highly racialised world'. The function of racism itself, she said, is 'distraction': 'It keeps you from doing your work. It keeps you explaining, over and over again, your reason for being.' This entire essay is about writing back to the white gaze. I need to write back to the white author who would steal my soul. I must prove I exist before I can exist.

Manning Clark saw no reason to question the fact of modernity, nor that Aboriginal people had no place in it. Like Thomas Keneally or William Stanner, the lauded historian lamented the inevitability of the passing of the blacks. The 'European theft of the land', Clark wrote, 'doomed the culture of the Aborigines, condemning them to destruction or degradation and the whites to peace, security and material success, at the price of a reputation in posterity for infamy'. Yes, the whites would be condemned but tomorrow would be theirs to live with their guilt. The blacks would have no tomorrow.

Fanon said that culture is 'marked off by fences and signposts'. This is how colonisers embed their power, but Fanon reminds us too that it is a 'defence mechanism', an 'instinct for preservation'. The colonised person must 'admit the inferiority of his culture . . . [and] recognise the unreality of his "nation"'. All white writing in Australia is an act of dispossession: an instinct for preservation. It is a claim on a story as sure as a fencepost is a claim on land. How can it not be? They are Australian writers only because this land was stolen from my ancestors. So it is that a white son of England is awarded the Nobel Prize in Literature for supposedly introducing a new continent to the world of letters. Imagine: a white transplanted Australian whose words on a page are lifted above sixty thousand-plus years of unending, unbroken story. It is Patrick White who speaks to the world about what it is to be this thing we call an Australian.

Between 2019 and 2020 I spent several months away from my country. Being overseas made me yearn for my home; as I always do, I turned to the familiarity of words and sounds: books and music that soothed my homesickness. By my bedside were works by Nam Le, Tony

Birch, Tara June Winch, Randolph Stow, David Malouf, Kim Scott, Katharine Susannah Prichard, Thomas Keneally, Christos Tsiolkas, Kate Grenville, Joan Lindsay and Patrick White. I read again White's *The Tree of Man*: the story of Stan Parker, who takes his new wife, Amy, into the Australian wilderness to hack out a new life; to breed a new people.

> Then the man took an axe and struck at the side of a hairy tree, more to hear the sound than for any other reason ... The silence was immense. It was the first time anything like this had happened in that part of the bush.

I read this and I see Stan Parker as Patrick White himself clearing the land for other white Australian writers to follow. For Christos Tsiolkas – whose parents' homeland was Greece – Patrick White was a 'way in'. Through White, Tsiolkas says he found a language to belong.

A way of making this place his own. In White's protagonist, Stan Parker, he sees a man coming to terms with exile; with isolation. Tsiolkas sees his own migrant father.

In his Writers on Writers essay on White, Tsiolkas calls *The Tree of Man* 'an origin story for the generations of settlers and migrants who have come to Australia seeking to create a new life'. Tsiolkas says it is not a foundation story for the first peoples of this country. That story, he says, is not White's to write. Oh, but it is, Christos. And it is yours to write. But you don't write it with an axe.

There is a lost continent that I imagine, a place where different stories are written. Where sovereignty resides in the First People; where we tell our stories in the first languages; where white writers don't say it is not their story to tell, but instead enter into that lore too because they did not come here with visions of emptiness but saw the people who were here and had been here since time immemorial. Where they respected the people who were here. We have never lived that country. We have never written that country.

White Australia has always written about us: defined us. It was white administrators and mission managers who divided us into categories, measuring our breeding like cattle: half-caste, quarter-caste, 'octoroon'. It was white welfare officers who decided whether parents could keep their children or who removed them to homes to become 'absorbed into the Commonwealth'. My great-aunt Eunice Grant slept in a dormitory with other black girls under a written sign demanding that she 'think white, act white, be white'. White people have never been reluctant to write about us. Tsiolkas is copping out: rather than looking to Patrick White for permission or an identity or to belong, why not look to the First Peoples to enter our tradition; to understand that story and his place in it before he writes a single word about what it is to be an 'Australian'?

As politicians make laws that constrain and define black lives, white writers consume black spaces. By giving names to people and places, they write over black spaces. By their presence, by their words, they erase black spaces. It is we who have to negotiate our return, or to withdraw; to withhold recognition. As the state exercises its claimed sovereignty, so white writers assume ownership of language and story. White writing is occupation: strangers writing themselves into existence in a foreign land they now presume to call their own. Writing is an expression of sovereignty. European languages scholar David Pan says world literature follows political sovereignty; it is a product of a liberal order and its accompanying universalism. Other traditions are swept aside. An axe strikes a tree, in a silent place.

White, like all Australian writers, wrote into the space of terra nullius. Historian Stuart

Macintyre says the story of Australia is of a 'sleeping land brought to life'. Sociologist Catriona Elder calls it the terra nullius narrative: 'non-Indigenous peoples could imagine they were telling a story where no other existed'. Aboriginal people were seen as incapable of surviving 'the onslaught of the modern world'. Blackness is excluded from the nation, Elder says, 'by Indigenous people being made white'.

In *Remembering Babylon*, David Malouf creates a white character as a black stand-in. Malouf's shipwrecked Gemmy spent years living with the blacks before stumbling back into white society. Through him, Malouf sees an Australia *becoming*: 'Our poor friend Gemmy is a forerunner. He is no longer a white man, or a European, whatever his birth, but a true child of this place as it will one day be.'

For this transformation to take place, though – Malouf warns us – the blacks must be removed. *Remembering Babylon* ends with the memory of a massacre. In his novel Malouf imagines this place working its changes on the people. Yet this is a white man (his Lebanese heritage aside, Malouf writes as a white Australian) writing about white people, in a place where blacks no longer have a speaking part.

Whatever Malouf's fancy of 'this place as it will one day be', modern Australia is resolutely, immovably a white country. It is conceived by the white imagination and its Enlightenment faith in progress and universalism. People were removed, like trees were removed, until whiteness prevailed. There was a time when Christos Tsiolkas the Greek was most certainly not 'white'. Through the power of story, he has become an Australian and assuredly white. Made so by his literary 'father' Patrick White. Tsiolkas enjoys the privilege of probing, poking, challenging multicultural (white) Australia from his assured place in it, because he writes in a place where blackness was removed by men with axes.

YOU CAN'T BE A BIT AND BIT

'And you seem to forget, my friend,

that there's no such thing as an Australian.

Except in the imagination of some poets . . .

The only true Australians are –'

At that moment he noticed Jimmie

waiting at the counter.

'– the aborigines,' he murmured . . .

'Jacko?' he called. 'He's an honest, poor

bastard but he's nearly extinct.'

'And, surprisingly, that is the work of

those you so fancifully call Australians.'

Thomas Keneally,

The Chant of Jimmie Blacksmith

The white poets who 'imagine' Australia into being can't escape their own illegitimacy; just like the nation they write about.

They know that a flag, an anthem, a constitution does not make a nation: a nation is a story, and their story can never be the story of this land; theirs will always be a stranger's story. It is no less profound, and these stories tell me something of who I am: we are a nation founded in theft and the brutal, tragic removal of a people. We are a remarkable nation, a hard-scrabble nation, a 'fair go' nation of immigrants, but that is a story we write after the great sin.

Keneally knows this, yet he is white and that is enough for him to assume in *The Chant of Jimmie Blacksmith* that he can enter our lives, our minds, our souls; change our names and speak for us even as he knows that his existence as an Australian comes at our cost. Australian writers are haunted by our absence. They look away or they look through us. We are a ghostly presence – a mystical reminder that Australian modernity is unstable. This is Freud's uncanny: when the familiar becomes strange; when home is not really home.

Tim Winton's *Cloudstreet* tells us Australians are haunted by possession. Literary scholar Michael Griffiths says the novel 'reflects the hauntedness of Australia as a settler-colonial nation-state'. The Pickles and Lambs are stalked by blackness: the spectre of the 'shadow girl' or the 'dark girl'. There is another ghost, an ugly white ghost: the spectre of white occupation. The white ghost is a reminder of the sickness of Australia – and it is sick, we lose sight of that; it is sick that we as a nation have never truly made peace with the people on whom we have inflicted and continue to inflict so much pain. We ask Aboriginal people to dance for us, paint for us, run for us, but we have never said to them: 'This is your country, may we live here, please?'

I have chosen to focus on Keneally's *Blacksmith* because it is so close to me, but I could have chosen *Cloudstreet* or Randolph Stow's *Tourmaline* or Joan Lindsay's *Picnic at Hanging Rock*. They work on me in similar ways: stories of people perishing or lost; grasping for somewhere to call home. Stow and Lindsay ponder the cost of conquering a land and destroying a people. They wonder whether the invaders will ever be at peace, or will this land devour them?

Both novels capture a foreboding that shimmers through this country like a mirage on the horizon. 'If you look at Tourmaline, shade your eyes . . . The road ends here.' Joan Lindsay's lost girls are a debt owed to the land. I have always thought of *Picnic at Hanging Rock* as a Dreaming story for white people. The girls form part of the landscape itself; are now inseparable from the rock. Those who remain are no longer British: so, what are they? Hungry ghosts, I suppose, feeding on a country that can never fill them up. Hungry ghosts are born of the lowest rung of hell, spawned by greed and desire and murder and theft. They will never die, but they will never know life either.

Stow and Lindsay write in a time in place and out of place. The postcolonial theorist Homi

Bhabha calls this 'the beyond', the 'in-between spaces'. I could have written about Eleanor Dark, who captured that sense of impermanence in her novel *The Timeless Land*. The 'mysterious beings with faces pale as bones' have come to this place. For people like Bennelong, these strangers mean the end of certainty. Captain Arthur Phillip, alone in his tent lit by a single candle, wonders at the 'utter strangeness of this land . . . the terra incognita'. It was as if England had never existed. Dark knew that blackness hovers over everything that is written in this country.

Those Indigenous writers by my bedside are trapped in a conversation with whiteness. They answer back to white people; they talk about white people. Whiteness matters far more than it should, but it is unavoidable. These black writers are what remains after invasion – stolen land, stolen people, stolen language – so they write about recovery:

their words, their culture, their family. They write about return. They are on a journey to discover themselves – discovery as rediscovery, Fanon said; they write to heal. To survive.

Gilles Deleuze said: 'One's always writing to bring something to life; to free life from where it's trapped.' Deleuze called it 'minority literature', meaning not that it is lesser but that it is written within a major language. Deleuze was talking about the Jewish Kafka and 'the impossibility of not writing, the impossibility of writing in German, the impossibility of writing otherwise'. That is the first thing to know: to speak back to power, we must use the language of the powerful. The second thing to know about minority literature: 'everything in them is political'. And third: 'everything takes on a collective value'. So it is for Aboriginal writers, writing in a language that supplanted the languages of our ancestors, to make the most political statement of all: that we are here and that we are bound to each other.

This should be a home for me. These black writers are my people in a way that the other Australian writers on my bedside table cannot be. And yet . . . I feel trapped here too. I feel compelled to choose in ways that suffocate me.

'You can't be a bit and bit. What are you, Noongar or wadjella?' (Kim Scott, *Kayang & Me*)

Noongar or wadjella? Black or white? Kim Scott knows he must pick a side. There can be no place in-between. As he wrote, 'I felt compelled to obey. There didn't seem to be any choice.' Scott's work is about excavation: digging up the past to find a trace of himself. Scott admits he did not grow up in Aboriginal culture; he had to go looking for it to find somewhere to belong. It is a common trope in Indigenous literature (and I'm uncomfortable even using that term because it assumes a homogeneity that erases our difference from each other): the search, the return home, to reclaim language or name. Identity is always located in the past. Like Jimmie Blacksmith, they are people estranged from their 'tribal' roots and not at home in the world.

Aboriginal people confront what anthropologist Elizabeth Povinelli calls the 'cunning of recognition': the need to prove we exist to a people who don't truly see us. We are called on to perform authenticity: to be recognised, we have to be recognisable. White Australia historically has defined what an Aboriginal person is. We must tick boxes and meet criteria of blood descent and community acceptance. I hate having to so definitively declare myself; it is not required of any other Australian. We are set a near-impossible task. The 1992 Mabo High Court decision is often hailed as a transformative moment that shattered the myth of terra nullius. It did no such thing. Native title exists within Australian law, not outside it. To be an acknowledged native title holder, Indigenous people have to prove an uninterrupted and continuing connection with their land in spite of colonisation. Australian law sees us only as people of the past.

Mabo has had a profound impact on Indigenous writers and Australian readers. White readers eager to reconcile with their history have embraced black storytellers. But on white terms. Among the most successful black writers are those who most resemble white Australia. They are fair-skinned suburbanites whose stories of a search for their roots appeal to white Australians who like to scour Ancestry.com. I want to be clear: I am not questioning the bona fides of these writers. I am one of them. I am aware that we open a space in the black world that white readers can enter.

White readers want to be healed, to be relieved of their burden of guilt. Truth-telling is invariably presented as a way of bringing white and black closer together. But it is truth without justice or consequences. Truth that comforts white Australia. The astonishing success of Sally Morgan's *My Place* in the 1980s created space for others to follow. These are identity novels like *The Yield* by Tara June Winch, which won the coveted Miles Franklin Award. Tara is a Wiradjuri person like me and her book echoes my family's story. Her novel tells of her protagonist's search for a Wiradjuri dictionary written by her 'grandfather'. As Tara acknowledges, she based this on the dictionary written by my father. The black 'family' in the novel live near Poison Waterholes Creek, also where my parents live. There is a subplot of the diary of a missionary inspired by the diary of John Brown Gribble, who established the Warangesda Mission on the banks of the Murrumbidgee River in south-west New South Wales, the mission where my great-grandmother was born.

Tara mentions my family in *The Yield* and our family trees wind around each other. Tara did not grow up on Wiradjuri country and her novel reads like an attempt to be seen, to locate herself on Wiradjuri land, in Wiradjuri story and Wiradjuri language. Yet for a story that is so close to my own, I don't recognise myself in her novel. She begins the book with a description of *ngurambang* – Wiradjuri land – she says when you say it you should taste blood in your words. I don't taste blood at all; I taste family and love. Tara tells her readers language 'is the way to all time, to time travel! You can go all the way back.' This is a novel for white people, and perhaps for those Aboriginal people removed from their communities. I can see how white people especially are seduced and comforted by the idea of someone returning to the past to find herself. If we can just go back, we can make the pain go away. But I want to live with all the pain; with all the broken bits. I want to live without certainty. We may share history, Tara and I, we may even share distant blood, but I don't share her idea of who we are. Being Wiradjuri is not something I rediscover; our language lives in the now, not in the then. But for Tara – like Thomas Keneally, like Kim Scott, like the judges of the High Court – being Aboriginal belongs to a time past, a connection severed and then recovered and rescued; a time before modernity and held out of reach of modernity. I respect Tara's success, and I feel the depth of her loss and her need to put it right. But I could not help feeling diminished by her novel, just as Keneally's *Blacksmith* leaves me diminished.

Bruce Pascoe says Aboriginal blood matters only as much as you want it to. It matters a lot to Pascoe. There are many Australians with Aboriginal ancestry who don't fashion that into an Aboriginal identity. Indeed, some may think it impertinent – if not offensive – to do so. Bruce Pascoe will tell you he lived the first half of his life as a white Australian. If DNA is a guide, he says, he is 'more Cornish than Koori'. He studied as a white person. He wrote as a white person. His work was critiqued by white reviewers. Pascoe was even criticised for lacking authenticity. Now he has embraced his oft-suspected but buried Indigenous ancestry.

Pascoe is a fascinating and unique writer. His book *Dark Emu: Black Seeds* has become a bestseller. *Dark Emu* has inspired a stage play, a children's edition, a TV documentary. He gives speeches and lectures and works in the academy as an Indigenous scholar. Pascoe is widely touted as Australia's most influential Indigenous historian. It is a role he seems to revel in, carefully cultivating his public image. His white hair has grown out, his beard is longer. He has an air of self-conscious mysticism, a Zen-like aura that I'm sure many believe adds to his authenticity. Pascoe has taken to being photographed with a red headband: a traditional signifier of the Aboriginal man of high degree. He has been criticised by some Aboriginal people for adopting a pantomime Aboriginality. It looks too much like putting on robes, playing dress-ups.

We all perform our identities to varying degrees, and I don't want to interrogate whether Bruce is or is not Indigenous. I have met him on several occasions, and I found him to be a good bloke. He has done some language work with my father. Dad speaks highly of Bruce and that's enough for me. If Bruce says he has Indigenous heritage, I have no reason to call him a liar. I understand, though, why some Aboriginal people are sceptical. They are wary of interlopers. These 'Jackies come lately' touch a raw nerve. Blackfellas have bitter memories. They recall their white-passing pale-skinned cousins crossing the street to avoid them. Those were hard times. Harsh discrimination and segregation laws meant Aboriginal heritage was frequently denied. Swarthy grandma was passed off as 'Spanish'. Of course some people made shameful decisions just to survive. Then there were those stolen from their families, and for their descendants it can be a long road home. Identity – who is and who isn't Aboriginal – is blackfella business. It is not Andrew Bolt's business.

I am much more interested in what Pascoe's success tells me about Australia. Pascoe is an 'invention' not unlike the way Jimmie Blacksmith was Keneally's invention. I was struck by something the historian Tom Griffiths wrote. He called Pascoe a 'storyteller in the old style'. Griffiths is not one to waste words. He is telling us something important: that the storyteller is different to the writer. Philosopher Walter Benjamin said, 'The storyteller's traces cling to a story the way traces of the potter's hand clings to a clay bowl.' That may be true too of the writer; the novelist. But the writer requires the reader and reading is a solitary experience; we may sometimes share it with others, but our deepest thoughts are ours alone. Who we are – our unique, individual desires, thoughts, dreams, fears, hopes, secrets, our imaginations – lift the written words off the page and give them life. The novelist is inseparable from the reader. The storyteller is the embodiment of the story itself. This personification is why people come to listen. The crowd falls under the storyteller's spell. The storyteller is transparent to the transcendent. The light on our dark path. The storyteller takes us to a land of magic and wonder to reveal essential truths. As Benjamin told us: 'The first true storyteller was and remains the teller of fairy tales.'

Pascoe is shrewd. I can see in him something of the old-time carny. He's a spruiker in a travelling medicine show. He is a conjurer. Pascoe invites people to disbelieve their eyes. The white man vanishes and behold, the black man appears. It doesn't work on Aboriginal people; we've seen it before. He seeks – and receives in some quarters – a black imprimatur. But he knows he has nothing new to reveal to us. This is an illusion for a white audience. Crucially, the conjurer is not a conman. Pascoe is not deceiving his audience. Far from it. They believe because they *want* to believe.

Pascoe knows this. Listen to how he describes his Aboriginal awakening: 'as if I have been led at night to a hill overlooking country I have never seen'. He is smart enough to play on the mythical archetype: the hero called to the forest, who must find the grail and return to save others. Pascoe has spun his own myth, replete with days in the wilderness; overturning the gatekeepers of received wisdom; his moment of revelation; and, crucially, his heroic return. He's had a vision and through him we can be led to his Australia never-never land.

Pascoe offers white Australians something they so desperately desire: absolution. Through him, they will see their country anew. In a speech at the Art Gallery of New South Wales, he said 'we have to find new ways of talking about the past'. Through him, the wounds of history will be healed. Just like him, his audience can connect more deeply to this place. They can even imagine themselves as Aboriginal people. Pascoe tells them belonging is in the land and the land is in us.

Tom Griffiths saw this up close. He was in a lecture hall with young people on a dark winter night all hanging on Bruce Pascoe's every word. They were enthralled. Griffiths said at the end of the speech they erupted in an ovation lasting several minutes. Griffiths doesn't say this, but he witnessed a transformation. Through the magic in the room Bruce Pascoe one-time white writer becomes Bruce Pascoe Aboriginal storyteller. As Walter Benjamin says, the 'storyteller assimilates what he knows . . . into all that he is'. The wick of the storyteller's life, Benjamin wrote, is 'entirely consumed by the gentle flame of his story'.

In 2016 I sat on the judging panel for the NSW Premier's Literary Awards, alongside Thomas Keneally, when Pascoe was nominated in the Indigenous writer category. Keneally and our fellow judge strongly supported Pascoe, but I resisted, arguing instead for the merits of Ellen Van Neerven's *Heat and Light*, a dazzling work of fiction I considered of greater depth and literary worth than *Dark Emu*. In the end we agreed that Pascoe and Van Neerven should share the prize. In any event, Pascoe went on to win the prestigious Book of the Year award. Perhaps my judgment was wrong. Of the two books, *Dark Emu* has certainly had the greater cultural impact.

The effect has been seismic. For many Australians *Dark Emu* shifted the ground beneath their feet. The book has been praised for deepening our understanding of and collective interest in the pre-colonial history of this land. *Dark Emu* is not an original work. Pascoe's 'revelation' that Indigenous people were the first bakers and early farmers has been no secret to those who have cared to look. Studying physical anthropology at university more than thirty years ago, I learned how the skeletal remains of Indigenous communities from Victoria's river system revealed traces of disease consistent with sedentary, settled lifestyles. They had formed fishing villages, lived more closely together, in greater numbers, in more permanent dwellings.

But *Dark Emu* is not an excavation of the past; it is a revelation of our present. Pascoe is the visibly white-skinned writer uncovering a buried Aboriginal past in the way he has uncovered his own buried heritage. He re-creates an Aboriginal utopia of verdant fields, miles of stooked grain, housing estates, roasting duck, industrious women happily baking while children play and men husband animals. He is saying to the white reader: 'Look, they were just like you': farmers, fishermen, bakers. Like Tara June Winch's *The Yield*, *Dark Emu* is a book embraced enthusiastically by white people. Indeed, it is a book written by white people: Pascoe's primary sources are the journals and observations of white 'explorers' and 'pioneers'.

Pascoe's Aboriginal society is seen through white eyes. The white witness is unimpeachable. Pascoe has often said that if white readers would not believe Aboriginal people, surely they will believe the white explorer. *Dark Emu* ceases to be Aboriginal history and becomes an Australian history: a foundational story in the growing narrative of a shared heritage. This Aboriginal agrarian society becomes visible to whiteness. Pascoe makes it accessible to white people. Are these Aboriginal people at all? Or are they proto-typically Australian?

In *Dark Emu*, Bruce Pascoe offers Australians the hope of a nation healed. *Dark Emu* is part of the project of reconciliation. It performs the function of a welcome to country: an act of generosity that offers settlers a more profound sense of belonging. And, just like being welcomed to country, it doesn't require white Australians to acknowledge Aboriginal sovereignty. I suspect that white people have flocked to *Dark Emu* because, like a welcome to country, it soothes them. It asks so little of them. It expiates their guilt because Aboriginal humanity – previously disparaged as savage and primitive, previously brutalised – now becomes something utterly familiar. 'Home' and 'hearth', as Jimmie Blacksmith said. With it, a man is 'beatified'.

FREE

Jimmie had left him native. Mort did not
see that – he would not be Mort and native
if he could. All he could sense was the love
and Jimmie's death.

Being native, he swallowed grief down
into his veins, where the festivals of mourning could proceed in the tides of his blood.

Thomas Keneally,

The Chant of Jimmie Blacksmith

Thomas Keneally says he would not write *The
Chant of Jimmie Blacksmith* in the same way today;
he would not inhabit an Aboriginal voice because
he could not imagine Aboriginal grief. He is right
about our grief. It is existential and total. It is a
grief for country and for our people. In a country where, statistically, Indigenous people die ten

years younger than the rest of the population, we remain in a permanent state of mourning. It is a grief beyond sadness. I have never found the English word that could describe it. Only the Korean word *han* gets close. It is more a feeling than a literal meaning. *Han* describes a deep sorrow, regret and anger. It comes from a long suffering of the Korean soul. No one who has not lived through our interminable loss could capture what it is to be Indigenous in Australia.

When Tom describes 'full-blood' Mort's grief for his 'half-caste' brother Jimmie, Tom sees something peculiarly 'native'; something Jimmie has lost. By abandoning Mort, Jimmie has made his choice: he will die as he lived, a man between worlds, and he will return Mort to the land; to his ritual and his spirit. Jimmie is a bastard and Mort is an Aborigine, but to Tom both are doomed.

Is Tom right? Should he not have written this book in this way? I don't believe him. It sounds disingenuous to me: too convenient; a get out of jail free card to avoid the identity police coming after him. Let me give him a break: Tom, I am glad you wrote it. Your book has stayed with me for forty years. It has changed as I have changed, and it has never failed to fascinate me. You spoke to the heart of a sixteen-year-old boy who was trying to find his way in the world. I felt the weight of my history, and in Jimmie's violence I felt a release: a charge of righteousness and anger. It was visceral and, from my vantage point now, irrational and poisonous. To a confused, sad, troubled and angry boy alive to the pain around him, and wondering why, Tom gave me a simple answer: it was the white man's fault.

Simple answers, I know now, are dangerous: make America great again; the century of humiliation; Brexit; restore the caliphate – simple answers are the solutions of demagogues. I don't deny their appeal. They speak to a wound of the soul; to a deep hurt and loss; to humiliation. Simple answers offer us a return to a golden age, but it is a toxic nostalgia. It shuts down our world, turns us inward. We become Mark Lilla's 'shipwrecked minds'.

I used to mistake grievance for justice. I held onto the pain of the past because it was the only weapon I had. Forgetting was betrayal. Anger was the iron in the blood of my identity. Jimmie Blacksmith was my talisman. Australia is deeply unjust still. It burns in me. I won't do your dance or put on your paint and play your didgeridoo. I won't perform for you. I won't conform to someone's idea of who or what I should be. I won't do that for white Australia or for black Australia. I will meet you face to face and demand to be seen. I won't tick your box or be put in your box. I won't carry the burden of your history. I will not give you my anger. I won't let you steal my future.

I don't believe in Jimmie Blacksmith anymore. I am not doomed. I am not caught between worlds. I have outgrown Tom's novel. But thank you again,

Tom, for writing it. Because of it, I see my country clearer. I see what you thought of us: that we were to be pitied, lamented, defended even; but that we were doomed. I am not doomed. I have survived and I am me: all of it born here; sixty thousand and two hundred years: black and white. I live now. I have no need of authors, black or white, who tell me I must go back to find myself, that I can become whole in language or country or history. If asked, I am Aboriginal – Wiradjuri, Kamilaroi – I cannot be white, that would be ludicrous. But as an Aboriginal person I turn my face to freedom: not the past. I turn my face to justice.

Don't tell me, Tom, that you would not write *Jimmie Blacksmith* today. Don't tell me it is not your place to write about Aboriginal people or in an Aboriginal voice. You have. In one of your recent books, *Two Old Men Dying*, you return us to the ancient Australia of the shores of Lake Mungo and the First People. You breathe life into Mungo Man – the oldest human remains ever uncovered in Australia. He is dynamic and he is real in ways that Jimmie Blacksmith wasn't. But Mungo Man lives 'before history', and Tom, you have no problem seeing us as people 'before history'. But you sent your Jimmie to the gallows as a man out of time; a man for whom history had no use.

Like me, Thomas Keneally made his own pilgrimage to the old Darlinghurst Gaol. Standing near where the real Jimmy Governor was hanged, he said he was sorry for 'assuming an Aboriginal voice'. He should have sought permission, he said. 'We can enter other cultures as long as we don't rip them off, as long as we don't loot and plunder,' he said. I don't think we can police our imaginations. I don't think we need to ask permission. Australian writers have never done this and, frankly, I see them and my country more clearly because of it. It is like the debate about Australia Day; why move the date if it will only hide the truth?

Tom said he came to the old Gaol to make peace with Jimmy Governor's ghost. So did I. For much of my life, I looked to Jimmy for the impossible: to tell me who I am. I would not let him escape history; I would not let his crimes die with him. I was so wrong. Jimmy lived in a world defined by black and white, and Tom Keneally kept him there. For the longest time, so did I. After standing on the spot where Jimmy was executed, I walked over to one of the art galleries. There, on a stained-glass window, one of the artists had painted Jimmy's face. It struck me then that in that kaleidoscope of colour – the explosion of blue and green and red and yellow – Jimmy was set free.

WORKS BY
THOMAS KENEALLY

FICTION

The Place at Whitton (1964)

The Fear (1965), rewritten in 1989 as *By the Line*

Bring Larks and Heroes (1967)

Three Cheers for the Paraclete (1968)

The Survivor (1969)

A Dutiful Daughter (1971)

The Chant of Jimmie Blacksmith (1972)

Blood Red, Sister Rose (1974)

Moses the Lawgiver (1975)

Gossip from the Forest (1975)

Season in Purgatory (1976)

Ned Kelly and the City of the Bees (1978)

A Victim of the Aurora (1977)

Passenger (1979)

Confederates (1979)

The Cut-Rate Kingdom (1980)

Schindler's Ark (1982)

A Family Madness (1985)

The Playmaker (1987)

Act of Grace (under the pseudonym
William Coyle, 1985)

Firestorm (1988)

Towards Asmara (1989)

Flying Hero Class (1991)

Chief of Staff (under the pseudonym
William Coyle, 1991)

Woman of the Inner Sea (1993)

Jacko: The Great Intruder (1993)

A River Town (1995)

Bettany's Book (2000)

An Angel in Australia (2000)

Office of Innocence (2002)

The Tyrant's Novel (2003)

Roos in Shoes (2003)

The Widow and Her Hero (2007)

The People's Train (2009)

The Daughters of Mars (2012)

Shame and the Captives (2014)

Napoleon's Last Island (2015)

Crimes of the Father (2016)

Two Old Men Dying (2018)

The Book of Science and Antiquities (2019)

The Dickens Boy (2020)

The Monsarrat series, co-authored with Meg Keneally

The Soldier's Curse (2016)

The Unmourned (2017)

The Power Game (2018)

The Ink Stain (2019)

NON-FICTION

Outback (1983)

Australia: Beyond the Dreamtime (1987)

The Place Where Souls Are Born:

A Journey into the American Southwest (1992)

Now and in Time to Be: Ireland and the Irish (1992)

Memoirs from a Young Republic (1993)

The Utility Player: The Des Hasler Story (1993)

Our Republic (1995)

Homebush Boy: A Memoir (1995)

The Great Shame (1998)

American Scoundrel: The Life of the Notorious Civil War

General Dan Sickles (2002)

Lincoln (2003)

The Commonwealth of Thieves:
The Story of the Founding of Australia (2005)
Searching for Schindler: A Memoir (2007)
Australians: Origins to Eureka (2009)
Three Famines: Starvation and Politics (2010)
Australians: Eureka to the Diggers (2011)
Australians: Flappers to Vietnam (2014)
Australians: A Short History (2016)

PLAYS
Halloran's Little Boat (1968)
Childermas (1968)
An Awful Rose (1972)
Bullie's House (1981)
Either Or (2007)

SCREENPLAYS
The Survivor (1972)
Silver City (1984)
The Fremantle Conspiracy (1988)